Bringing the Farmhouse Home

by Gloria Whelan
illustrated by Jada Rowland

SIMON & SCHUSTER BOOKS FOR YOUNG READERS
Published by Simon & Schuster
New York   London   Toronto   Sydney   Tokyo   Singapore

SIMON & SCHUSTER BOOKS FOR YOUNG READERS
Simon & Schuster Building, Rockefeller Center
1230 Avenue of the Americas, New York, New York 10020.
Text copyright © 1992 by Gloria Whelan
Illustrations copyright © 1992 by Jada Rowland
All rights reserved including the right of reproduction
in whole or in part in any form.
SIMON & SCHUSTER BOOKS FOR YOUNG READERS
is a trademark of Simon & Schuster.
Designed by Vicki Kalajian.
The text of this book is set in 15 pt. Berkeley Old Style.
The illustrations were done in watercolor, pen and ink.

Manufactured in Hong Kong

10 9 8 7 6 5 4 3 2 1

Library of Congress Cataloging-in-Publication Data
Whelan, Gloria. Bringing the farmhouse home / by Gloria Whelan;
illustrated by Jada Rowland. Summary: When Grandma dies,
her five children and their children descend on her farmhouse
to divide the possessions in an orderly manner and in hopes
of making everyone happy. [1. Death—Fiction.
2. Inheritance and succession—Fiction. 3. Family life—Fiction.] I. Rowland,
Jada, ill. II. Title. PZ7.W5718Br 1992 [E]—dc20 CIP 91-16411
ISBN 0-671-74984-6

For David Barr
— GW

To my sisters and brothers
(-in-law, too)
— JR

The summer after my grandma died, my aunts and uncles and cousins came to her farmhouse from all over. Uncle Charlie and Aunt Kate pulled up in a green truck. Aunt Helen and Uncle Al and my cousins Freddie and Ruth and Norma came in an old bus with ruffled curtains at the windows. We borrowed a trailer to hitch on to our car.

Uncle Bill and Aunt Ellie and Shirley, who is just my age, and Uncle John and Aunt Edna and little Tom were already there. They were waiting for us on the front porch.

Now that Grandma was gone, the farmhouse was going to be sold. I remembered all the good times I had visiting there—baking cookies with my grandma and playing hide-and-seek in the barn with my cousins and gathering eggs still warm from the hens.

All the things in the farmhouse would be shared out
among my mother and her two sisters and two brothers.
"How will you do that?" I asked my mother.
"We'll divide everything into five piles," Mom said, "one pile
for each one of Grandma's children. Then we'll draw lots."

"We'll make the piles as even as we can," Dad said, "because we don't know which one we'll draw."

Everyone was hurrying from room to room. They were poking through cupboards and drawers, and running up and down the stairs. They were looking for their favorite things.

Aunt Ellie said that she hoped she would
draw the rocking chair my grandpa had made.

Uncle Bill wanted the family Bible with all
of our names written in it. In ink!

Mother set her heart on a platter with pink and
red roses painted on it. "Your grandmother always
served our birthday cakes on that platter," she said.

Aunt Edna said, "That platter is my favorite, too."

My cousin Shirley said that she would like to
have the painting of the lake with the moon
shining on the water. My cousin Tom wanted
the cuckoo clock.

I began to look for something, too.
There were the lace doilies Grandma
crocheted, delicate as frost on a window.
There was the yellow bowl, so big I
couldn't get my arms around it, that
Grandma used to mix the cookie dough.
There was the little box that held
Grandma's ring with a real pearl and
Grandpa's gold cuff links. The box had
forget-me-nots painted on it.

Then I saw Grandma's quilt. The quilt had a patch
from the apron Grandma wore when she baked cookies
and another patch from Grandpa's shirt. There was a
patch from the flowered pink dress Grandma had sewed
for me the Christmas before last.

"Mom," I whispered, "couldn't we have the quilt?"
"If we're lucky enough to draw the pile that it's on,"
said my mother.

"All right," called Aunt Kate. Dad says Aunt Kate has a voice you can hear two counties away. "All the children into the kitchen and keep out of our way. The grown-ups have work to do."

They began to heap things onto the five piles.

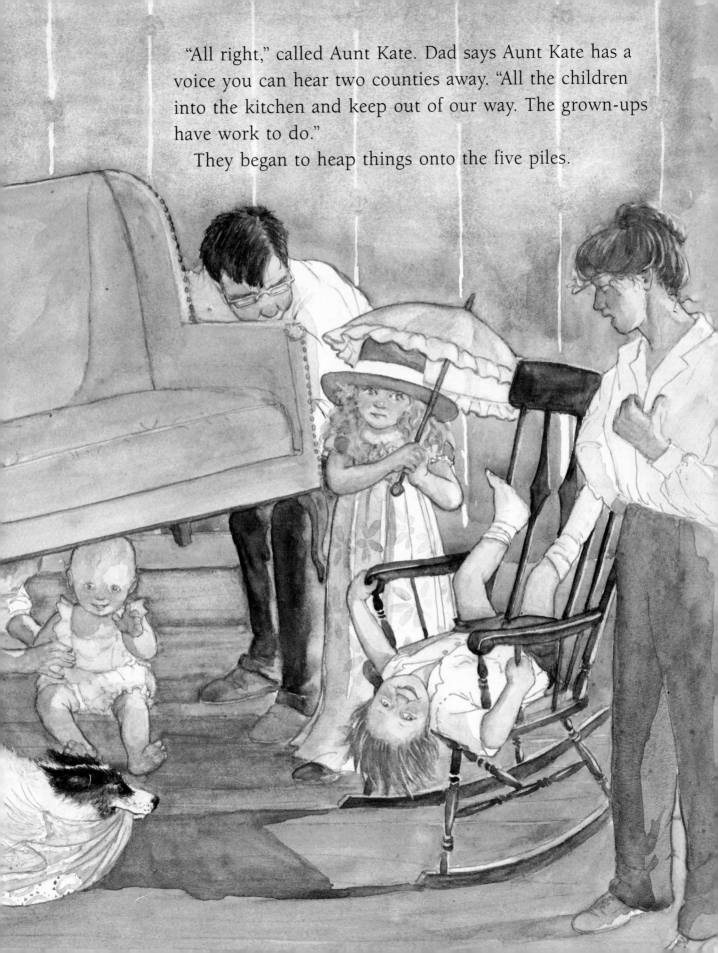

In the kitchen my cousins and I arranged the chairs into
a row and played Button, Button, Who's Got the Button?
and My Father Owns a Drugstore and Giant Steps.

We kept peeking into the living room, where my parents and all my aunts and uncles were bustling about collecting furniture and dishes. The piles were growing as high as mountains.

"That pile over there is skimpy," Aunt Helen warned.

Uncle Charlie added an oak table to the pile.

The family album with the pictures of my mother and aunts and uncles when they were babies without clothes on went on one pile. A pillow that was stuffed with pine needles and smelled just like a forest went on another.

Finally, Uncle Al called, "Attention everyone. Time out for dinner!"

Each family had brought a hot dish. I had Aunt Ellie's sweet potatoes with little marshmallows and Aunt Edna's five-bean salad and Uncle John's ham with pineapple slices and brown sugar on top and two helpings of my mother's pear crumble pie.

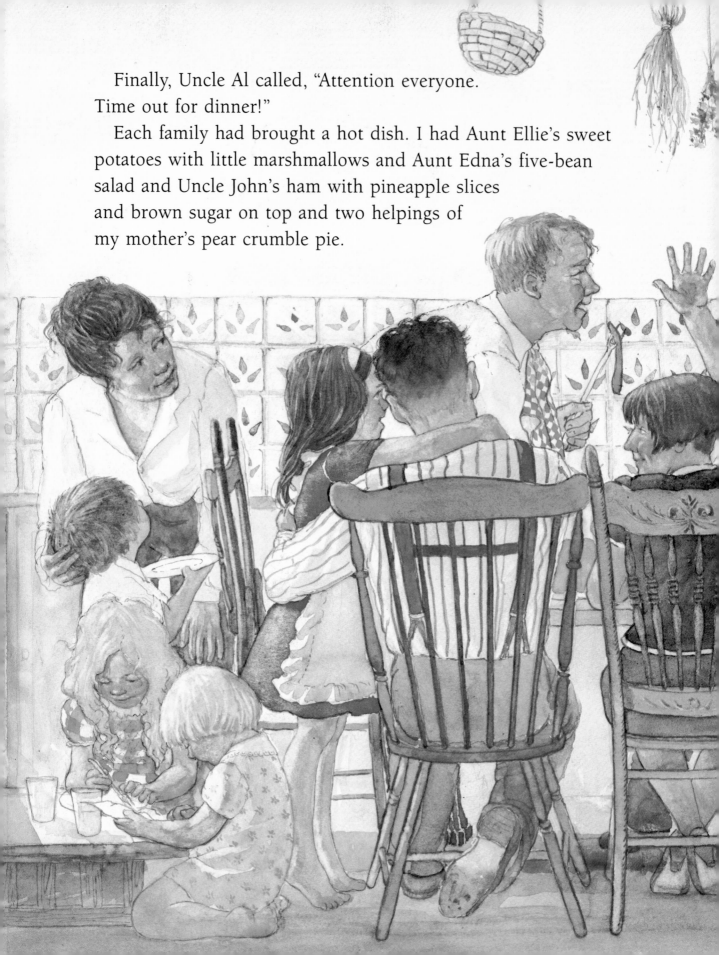

We ate and ate.

"I'm too full to move," my dad said, but Uncle John started picking up the chairs right from under us and heaved them onto the piles.

My cousins and I ran to look. Each pile had a piece of paper with a number on it.

I went from pile to pile looking for the quilt. It was on pile number five on top of my grandpa's fishing poles.

My Uncle Bill said, "Well, folks, I guess we're all ready."
Uncle Bill had five slips of paper in his hand. They
were folded up so you couldn't see the numbers. For the
first time that day, things got quiet. Each one of my
grandma's sons and daughters chose a slip of paper.

My mother drew number four. "It's my lucky day," she
said. "I've got the platter with the roses."

I sneaked a look to see who had drawn the quilt. It was Aunt Edna. I didn't cry, but I felt like it.

Mom squeezed my hand. "It's not over yet, Sarah. You may still have a chance. Wait and see what happens next."

"All right," Aunt Kate called. "Let's begin the trading, but remember, we're all ladies and gentlemen."

I guess they forgot, because everyone started to run
around like crazy, shouting at one another.

"I'll give you the rocking chair for the Bible,"
Uncle Charlie called to Aunt Ellie.

"Bill, how about trading me the cuckoo clock for that
picture your dad painted?" Uncle John asked Uncle Bill.

When they were through, half of the things on the
piles had been exchanged. But the quilt was still on
Aunt Edna's pile.

"Mom," I whispered, "couldn't you trade Aunt Edna something for the quilt?"

"Edna," my mother said, "I'll give you Dad's gold cuff links for the quilt."

"Sorry, Susie," Aunt Edna said, "but there's only one thing that means more to me than the quilt. It's Mom's platter with the roses."

Mom went all quiet. Then she looked at me. "All right. Here it is, Edna," she said, and held out the platter.

Aunt Edna handed her the quilt and said, "You can borrow the platter, Susie, any time you want to." Aunt Edna gave Mom a kiss.

I hugged the quilt. It smelled of the lavender in
Grandma's garden.

We began to load up our things to take them away.

A lamp stuck out of the bus window. A rocking chair was tied to the roof of a car. Our trailer was piled right up to the top.

We said good-bye. Everyone got kissed and hugged. Then we all took the farmhouse home.